C000017683

COCKTAILS

COCKTAILS

Thomas Kelly

Eagle
Editions

AN OCEANA BOOK

Published by Eagle Editions Ltd
11 Heathfield
Royston
Hertfordshire SG8 5BW

Copyright ©MCMXCIX Quantum Publishing
This book printed 2000

All rights reserved.
This book is protected by copyright. No part of it may be
reproduced, stored in a retrieval system, or transmitted in
any form or by any means, without the prior permission in
writing of the Publisher, nor be otherwise circulated in any
form of binding or cover other than that in which it is
published and without a similar condition including this
condition being imposed on the subsequent publisher.

ISBN 1-86160-374-6

This book was designed and produced by
Oceana Books
The Old Brewery
6 Blundell Street
London N7 9BH

Project Manager : Rebecca Kingsley
Designer : Wayne Humphries
Editor: Clare Howarth-Maden

QUMCCKT

Typseset in Gill Sans
Manufactured in Singapore by Eray Scan Pte Ltd
Printed and bound in Singapore by Star Standard Ind Pte Ltd

Credits
Thanks to all at Freud in London for their co-operation and
for mixing the drinks.

CONTENTS

Introduction

A 'cocktail' is a generic term for a mixed drink and has become synonymous with an alcoholic drink. There are numerous different versions of the story of the historical evolution of cocktails. The first cocktail-recipe books were written in the 1800s and cocktails appear to have become fashionable in about the 1870s. The cocktail really came to prominence during the Prohibition era in the United States of America. Since then, the image of cocktails has gradually developed, often as a result of the influence of movies.

Originally, cocktails were a way of enhancing the taste of a drink by mixing various combinations of flavours. During the Prohibition era cocktails were used to disguise the taste of bootleg liquor. Following the raising of the Prohibition, cocktails became fashionable and they continued to develop slowly. During the 1970s appearance became important, the cocktail often looking like a colourful part of the rain forest. By the late 1970s there was a revival in the fashion for cocktails. Since then there has been a gradual expansion of the world of cocktail-making, cocktails incorporating alcohol from all over the world. Cocktails can now be found as an added feature in basic recipe books, and there are also numerous specialist books available.

There are now over 10,000 recognised cocktails from all the world and this figure is always increasing. Yet at the same time there are standard themes that link various cocktails. There are various bartenders' guilds or associations, but your average cocktail bartender is unlikely to be a member of any of them.

The world of cocktails can be very confusing. The aim of this book is to give you a basic introduction to the art. It is not intended to swamp you with a mass of recipes, but rather to give you a clear understanding of the basic principles of cocktail-making.

Making cocktails is easy. Inventing good cocktails is slightly more difficult. However, once you have mastered the basic principles of cocktail-making it is relatively easy to reproduce most types of cocktail using the details about a cocktail's ingredients which are frequently detailed in the cocktail menus of bars.

Whenever you go to a bar, you should also squeeze as much information as you can out of the bartender and watch what he or she does. Most bartenders are happy to discuss their job with you and will always explain the ingredients that are contained in any drink that they are serving you.

Anyone can invent a cocktail. There are a large number of traditional cocktail recipes, but some of the best cocktails are the ones that were originally made on the spur of the moment. At the end of the day, we all have different tastes. Even the recipes for the various drinks that are regarded as 'classics' may vary according to the compiler's taste.

The most important rule that you should remember is that cocktail-making should be fun.

Golden rules

There are a few golden rules that I recommend to anyone making cocktails for the first time.

1. Start with simple cocktails. Make sure that you enjoy making cocktails and let your confidence grow before trying to tackle the more difficult recipes or invest in expensive equipment.

2. Slowly build up your stock of liquors. When doing so, learn to recognise the taste of each liquor.

3. Should you want to try a cocktail which contains a liquor that you do not own, it may be more sensible to try the cocktail in a bar or restaurant first, to make sure that you like the taste, before buying a bottle.

4. Start small. Your first cocktail party should include only you and one or two friends. Move on to larger audiences and events only when you have become more confident in your cocktail-making ability.

5. Everyone can make a bad cocktail. Until you are sure of your abilities always measure out the ingredients. If it does not suit your taste then play with the recipe until you are happy with it.

In this book I have tried to ensure that each chapter can stand alone, so that reference does not have to be made to other parts of the book. If some repetition occurs as a result, then I apologise.

Measurements

The measurements that I have used in this book are based upon the European fluid ounce. This is approximately 1.04 times the size of the American fluid ounce. For those who work in metric, rather than imperial measures, 1 fl oz is roughly 25 ml. The most important thing is to ensure that the proportions of the ingredients are correct.

During my time as a bartender people would often ask for a 'good' pour, expecting more alcohol for their money. Doing this, however, totally ruins the taste of most cocktails. We used to get round this by putting our thumbs over the air holes of the pour spouts so that the liquid would take longer to pour and thus make the customer believe that they were getting more alcohol. Indeed, the grateful customer would often tip extra for exactly the same drink that everyone else was getting.

Another thing to remember about measurements is that people should know roughly how much alcohol they are drinking, both for social purposes and to prevent them drink-driving. The drinks in this book contain roughly 1.5 to 2.25 fl oz of alcohol. It is impossible to give accurate measurements of alcoholic content for each drink as different spirits have different strengths. Avoid the temptation to 'spike' someone's drink or to get them to drink beyond their limit. It is not so funny when the ambulance arrives to take them away.

Terminology

Blend

The drink is made in a blender. The ingredients are placed in the blender in the order listed and then blended together until smooth. The drink is of the proper consistency when a line appears across the centre of the drink whilst blending and when a straw can stand in the drink unsupported.

Build/built

The drinks are poured straight into the glass in the order listed.

Chilled

When using sturdy glassware, the glass can be placed in the freezer until it is cold. When it is removed from the freezer a frost will appear on the glass. For thinner, more delicate glasses, place ice in the glass along with water or soda water. Leave it until it is chilled and then throw the ice and water away, shaking the excess out of the glass before pouring in the drink.

Dash

Quarter of a teaspoon of the ingredient.

Frozen

The drink contains ice cream, sorbet and/or crushed ice blended together.

Layer

The idea is to obtain separate layers in the drink. This is achieved by pouring the ingredients slowly onto the top of the drink and is often assisted by pouring the ingredient over the back of a spoon.

Mix

The drink is poured into the bottom of a cocktail-shaker and mixed with a Hamilton Beach blender.

On the rocks

The drink is served in a glass with ice.

Shaken

The drink is poured into a cocktail-shaker and shaken before being poured into the glass. In general, when the drink is to be poured into a chilled glass it is shaken with ice and strained into the glass. When the drink is to be poured into a glass containing ice, on the other hand, then it is shaken without ice.

Splash

For alcohol, approximately two drops of the ingredient. For fruit juice or soda, a quick splash from the container.

Stir

Simply pour the drink into a glass and then stir the ingredients together gently until they are well combined.

Straight up

The drink is served in a glass without ice. The drink may be served at room temperature or chilled.

Basic ingredients

I have not sought to provide an extensive guide to all the various spirits available. To do so would take far too long. The aim of this list is to give you a general guide to the ingredients which you will be using in this book. The most important points to remember for any ingredient are its flavour and the other ingredients that it mixes with. A lot of this knowledge will come with experience, but I have tried to give you an idea of the flavour of each ingredient.

Amaretto: an almond-flavoured liqueur with a hint of apricot in it.

Angostura bitters: a secret blend of vegetables and spices with a basic flavour of gentian.

Bailey's Irish Cream: an Irish liqueur made from cream, Irish whiskey and chocolate, giving it a distinctively sweet, creamy, chocolate flavour – this should not be mixed with acidic or citric ingredients.

Blue Curaçao: a blue version of triple sec with a distinctly orange taste.

Brandy: a strong, distilled wine matured in an oak cask to give it a distinctly smoky flavour.

Cherry brandy: a cherry-flavoured liqueur made by macerating fruit in brandy.

Crème de Bananes: a banana-flavoured liqueur made by macerating bananas in spirit.

Crème de Cacao: a sweet liqueur with a strong cocoa-vanilla flavour.

Crème de Cassis: a blackcurrant-flavoured liqueur made by macerating blackcurrants in spirit.

Cognac: a more refined version of brandy.

Cointreau: a popular French triple sec with a basic

flavour of sweet oranges, which is slightly sweeter than other triple secs that you will come across.

Drambuie: a liqueur made from Scotch whisky and honey, giving it a distinctively sweet taste.

Frangelico: an Italian liqueur tasting of hazelnuts.

Galliano: a golden liqueur with a herb base and tasting of sweet vanilla.

Gin: a neutral grain spirit which is flavoured with a number of ingredients, but with a predominant taste of juniper berries.

Grand Marnier: a cognac-based liqueur tasting of orange with a slightly dry aftertaste.

Grenadine: a sugar syrup tasting of pomegranates. This may be alcoholic or non-alcoholic.

Jack Daniels: a Tennessee sour-mash whisky made from a distillation of corn, rye and barley. Sour-mash whisky has a very strong, smoky taste.

Kahlua/Tia Maria: two variations on the same theme. Both have a coffee taste. Kahlua is a Mexican coffee liqueur, while Tia Maria is a Jamaican version with a rum base.

Malibu: a Jamaican, rum-based, coconut-flavoured alcoholic liqueur.

Martini: a fortified wine made in a number of distinctive flavours.

Midori: a green, melon-flavoured liqueur.

Orgeat: an almond-flavoured, non-alcoholic, sugar syrup.

Peach Schnapps: a peach-flavoured spirit.

Peppermint Schnapps/Crème de Menthe: a grain-based spirit tasting of sweet peppermints. It can be either colourless or a green, clear liquid.

Pimms: there are a number of varieties of Pimms, the most popular being No 1 cup. It has a gin base and contains a blend of liqueurs and fruit extracts, giving it a distinctive, bitter-sweet, fruity flavour.

Rum: a molasses-based liqueur matured in an oak barrel to give it a distinctively dry taste. Dark rum is coloured with caramel and has a slightly sweeter taste.

Sambuca: an Italian after-dinner liqueur tasting of aniseed.

Scotch whisky: a grain liqueur, distilled from fermented barley and flavoured in an oak cask. The distinctive colour is produced by adding caramel, whisky being a colourless liquid. Different areas produce different flavours of whisky, from a slightly smoky to a heavy peat flavour. Blended whiskies are a combination of whiskies blended to give a uniformly light, smoky taste. Only blended Scotch whiskies should be used in cocktails as a single malt whisky is likely to smother the overall taste.

Sloe gin: a liqueur made by macerating sloe berries in gin. It tastes of sloe and juniper berries.

Southern Comfort: a whisky-based drink flavoured with peach, orange and herbs. It tastes of sweet, fruity whisky.

Tequila: produced from the distillation of a fruit known as the pina, which comes from the mezcal plant, tequila has a distinctive flavour which is almost impossible to describe. I am afraid that you will have to try this one yourself.

Triple sec: the most basic form of Curaçao. It is a colourless liqueur made by infusing the bitter peel of the Curaçao orange with grape brandy, giving it a sweet, orange flavour.

Vodka: a smooth grain spirit tasting of pure alcohol.

Substitutes

It is unrealistic to expect you to have every ingredient to hand right from the start. At the same time, some ingredients, such as orgeat, can be very difficult to get hold of. In straitened circumstances it is acceptable to substitute fruit or fruit syrup for the fruit flavours contained by certain spirits. This is also an acceptable way in which to turn an alcoholic cocktail into a 'virgin', or non-alcoholic, cocktail.

Amaretto is an acceptable substitute for orgeat.

Kahlua and Tia Maria taste practically the same in a cocktail and therefore whichever you use is a matter of personal preference. Their taste can be simulated with ground coffee, but it is very difficult to get the proportions right.

As a substitute for any form of Curaçao I suggest that you use triple sec, as the others all impart distinctive colours to the drink and may leave you with an interestingly coloured cocktail.

Vodka has no substitute and does not really need one. It gives a bite to a drink, but in most recipes its flavour is masked by the other ingredients so it could therefore be left out.

Frangelico's taste may be simulated using hazelnuts and a simple syrup.

It is not possible to simulate the tastes of brandy, whisky or other such drinks, and without these ingredients it is impossible to reproduce the relevant cocktails properly.

Garnishes

The purpose of a garnish is either to enhance the taste of the drink, to enhance the appearance of the drink or both. Garnishes should be discreet and should not hinder the transfer of the cocktail from the glass to the mouth. When garnishes are used you should also supply drinking straws to prevent the consumer having to fight the garnish to get to the drink. The best straws to use are larger-width straws, such as you find in hamburger restaurants.

Simple garnishes do not require any real preparation beforehand. However, garnishes can be prepared in advance and kept in a container in the fridge for up to two days. Citrus fruits are best stored in soda water to prevent them drying out. Other fruits are best kept in clingfilm, while fruits like bananas should never be kept in the fridge.

Throughout this book you will be advised of the garnish which best suits each individual drink. When the garnish is squeezed into the drink or comprises a rim on the glass, it forms part of the overall flavour, and it is therefore important that the drink is made with that garnish. When the garnish is placed on the rim of the glass it is primarily for ornamental purposes and the drink can be made without it.

The most common types of garnish

Cherry: this can either be dropped straight onto the top of the drink or speared onto a slice of fruit using a cocktail stick or sword. The cherry rarely forms part of the taste of the drink and can usually be left out if necessary.

Rim: this can be made of either salt or sugar. A bar will have sponges of lime juice (salt) or water (sugar) to dip the glass in. In the absence of these you can produce the same effect by placing a small amount of the appropriate fluid in a shallow plate and dipping the glass into it. The base of a salt rim can also be set up by wiping a piece of lime around the top of the glass. A rim is supposed to be delicate and should not smother the taste of the drink. Dip the glass lightly into the liquid and shake off any excess. Then dip the top of the glass into the salt or sugar and lightly shake off the excess to prevent it dropping into the drink.

Slice: the fruit is cut lengthwise. For larger fruits, such as pineapples, cut the fruit into quarters. For smaller fruits, such as oranges, cut the fruit in half. The fruit is then sliced crossways into thin slices which should be thick enough to support the fruit but not so large as to take over the drink. The slice is placed on the side of the glass and a slit should be cut about 1 cm into the centre of the slice.

Bananas are cut diagonally across to produce a 1.5 to 2 cm slice which is pushed onto the rim of the glass.

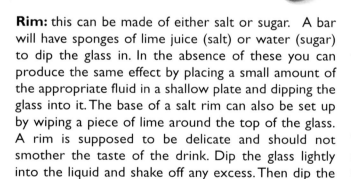

Squeeze: to prepare a squeeze you need a wedge of the appropriate fruit. This is prepared by cutting the fruit lengthwise into sixths or eighths, depending on the size of the fruit. The fruit is squeezed into the drink and the remains are dropped onto the top of it.

Twist: cut the end off the fruit. Then take a knife and score the skin from top to bottom in thin slices, about 0.5 cm wide, being careful not to cut through to the flesh of the fruit. Then take a spoon and push it under the skin from the open end, separating the skin from the fruit. The twist is a strip of the skin, pulled off the fruit. It is twisted to squeeze out the juices and then wiped around the rim of the glass before being dropped into the glass on top of the drink.

Basic tools

1 Glass (highball)
2 Strainer
3 Bar spoon
4 Sharp knife
5 Teaspoon
6 Measuring cups
7 Pouring spout
8 Chopping board

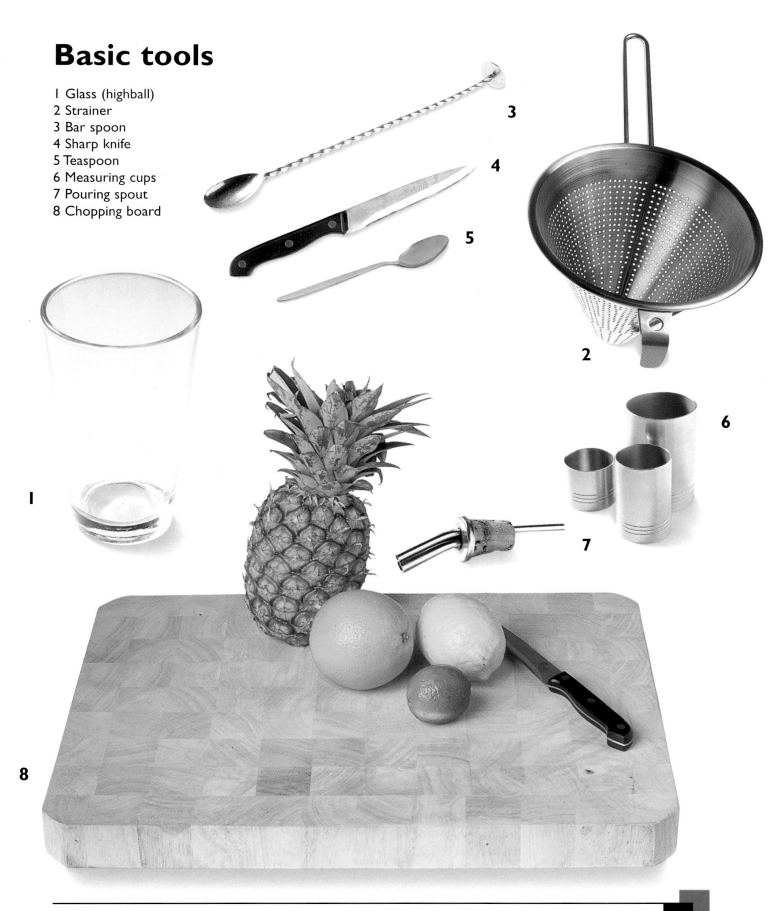

Mixers

Most mixers can be purchased from your supermarket or local shop, and I do not intend to insult your intelligence by trying to tell you either what goes into them or describing the taste of mixers like bitter lemon, soda water or tonic water.

I have given you the recipes for a Pina-colada mix and a Bloody Mary mix in this book. Here I shall deal solely with any additional mixes that you may need.

Half and half: this is half double cream and half milk mixed together. Should you be worried about your waistline, then you can substitute semi-skimmed milk in long drinks, but not in blended drinks.

Lime mix: this is a packet mix used in restaurants and bars in place of fresh lime juice. I would suggest that you only use this when catering for large groups.

Margarita mix: this is a base mix which can be used in margaritas in place of lime juice. It is made up by mixing a 12 fl oz can of limeade, best purchased frozen, with 2 fl oz Rose's lime juice.

Simple syrup: this is sugar dissolved in water. The basic proportion is 0.5 kg of sugar to 1 litre of water. Add the sugar gradually and stir to mix. The sugar will dissolve more quickly if the water is warm.

Sweet and sour: this is a packet mix which is used in restaurants and bars in place of lemon juice. It is especially good in iced teas, but can be difficult to obtain.

Glassware

To start off with, you can probably make do with whatever glassware you have available. However, as you progress, you will probably consider expanding your glass collection. Throughout this book I have indicated what glassware you will need.

Accidents will happen in any bar, and glassware will be broken. Sudden changes in temperature will also cause some glassware to break. As a general rule it is better to buy thicker glassware. Avoid anything crystal and always work on the basis that whatever you use is likely to be broken sooner or later.

There are obvious instances when breakages are likely, so you should try to take extra care. When pouring a blended drink into a glass, for example, if the drink will not pour easily, slap the side of the blender with your hand to shake the drink about. Never tap the blender on the rim of the glass to force the drink out of the blender.

Glasses should rarely be chilled in a freezer. I usually recommend this only for the thickest glassware, such as goblets.

Always consider warming or cooling the glass first. With hot drinks, either place a metal spoon or some cold water at the bottom of the glass before adding hot water. With frozen drinks, put a few ice cubes in the glass beforehand to lower the temperature. Both methods have the added benefit of keeping the drink 'fresh' for longer.

The size of the glasses given in the following recipes is only an indicator. Should you have different-sized glassware then you can just adjust the recipe accordingly whilst maintaining the same proportions. Most drinks can be served in a variety of glassware. The most important point to remember is that the glassware should be clean.

Anatomy of a cocktail

There is rhyme and reason behind most things that we do. Making cocktails is no different. This chapter sets out the basic rules to follow when recreating or inventing cocktails.

There are two aspects to all cocktails: the base and the mix. The base will usually be a combination of one primary liquor with smaller amounts of other liquors, but may also be equal amounts of a number of liquors. The mix is usually half and half or a combination of fruit juices, but a mix is not always required.

Base

The combination of liquors that form the base will depend upon the number of liqours to be included. As a standard guideline, in a drink containing more than one liquor the total amount of alcohol in a drink will be about 2 to 2.25 fl oz.

Most cocktails will have 1.25 fl oz of the main liquor and the remainder of the content will be divided equally between the rest. Alternatively, the amount of each liquor can be the same. It is rare to have a liquor base with differing amounts of each ingredient.

You will usually find that the main liquor is the one with which you are the most familiar, such as vodka, Scotch whisky and gin. The main liquor will define the character of the drink.

Mix

The contents of the half and half have already been dealt with in the Mixers section.

There is no guiding principle when mixing fruit juices. Most juices will combine to form an acceptable mix. When tasting, if you are aware of the contents of the mix then you will usually find that it includes equal measures of the main juices, with smaller amounts of such ingredients as grenadine, angostura bitters and syrup.

Blended drinks

These will usually have a slightly lower alcoholic content; approximately 1.25 to 2 fl oz of liquor. When the drink is blended with ice cream, it will not have a fruit base. When it is blended with sorbet, it will not have a milk or cream base. With crushed ice, either base may be used.

Shooters

These will often consist only of the liquor base, with no mixer. They will contain around 1.5 fl oz of liquor and the liquor is usually split in equal quantities between the different ingredients.

Long drinks

These follow the basic principles set on page 18.

Short drinks

These have a much smaller amount of mix than long drinks, but often contain the same amount of liquor.

Ways to serve

Frozen
The base is blended with crushed ice.

Ice cream
The base is blended with ice cream until there is a smooth consistency.

On the rocks
The drink is served in a glass with ice cubes.

Sorbet
A variation on ice cream, using frozen sorbet instead.

Straight up
The drink is served in a glass without ice. Often the glass and drink are chilled beforehand.

Ice

It will probably come as no surprise that ice is intended to make the drink cold. However, the amount of ice used in a drink can have a drastic effect on the taste.

Unless otherwise stated, when the drink is already cold before it is poured into the glass then the ice should come up to about 0.5 cm from the top of the glass. When the drink is not cold before it is poured into the glass then the ice should come up to the top of the glass, with about three or four cubes showing over the rim.

My customers used to think that they would get more drink if they had less ice in their glasses and would often ask me not to put ice into their drinks. They would then be disappointed when the drink was served in a smaller glass. Alternatively, they would ask for less ice, but this would ruin the taste of the drink. You need a high ratio of ice to drink to keep the drink cold and tasting right. A lower ratio means that whatever ice there is in the drink is more likely to melt, leaving a warmer, watered-down drink.

Basic bar

At the start of each chapter I will be guiding you through the equipment which you will need for the drinks that follow. However, there are some items that are required in every case, as follows.

Measuring

You will need something with which to measure out the ingredients. Bartenders usually use jiggers or pour spouts.

A jigger is a spirit measure, usually made of metal. The ingredient is poured into the jigger, then into the drink. The jigger is the most common type of measuring device used when optics are not fitted to the bottle.

Pour spouts are spouts inserted into the top of the bottle which regulate the flow of the liquor. The measure is taken by counting, with 0.25 fl oz being poured for every count. When the bottle is turned over, additional time is taken for the liquor to start to pour and the count therefore goes 'Bubble, two, three' and so on.

Common household implements that can be used instead are measuring spoons, standard spoons, small glasses or even the tops of some bottles. The main thing is to ensure that the proportion of the ingredients is correct.

Mixing

The most basic way of mixing a drink is to pour it into the glass and stir it with a spoon. A bar spoon is a long-handled spoon that is especially suited to this purpose, but any spoon will do.

The next stage is the shake. Ideally, you should use a cocktail-shaker. Most cocktail-shakers come with a top and an in-built strainer. Avoid cocktail-shakers that have fancy gadgets, such as one I recently encountered that had various cocktail recipes printed on the side that were accessed by twisting the inside of the shaker round a sleeve.

To improvise a cocktail-shaker, you need a thick glass, such as a large highball glass, and a metal shaking tin, which can be obtained from the kitchenware department of any large department store. The shaking tin should fit over the top of the glass and they are pushed together before the shaking is done. This is the basis of the 'Boston' shaker. However, in my experience the glass will often break, especially when you are trying to separate the two. To strain the drink, you will need either a proper strainer or you can separate the two slightly so that the drink pours out but the ice stays in.

Glassware should be kept clean and polished. When making a drink, your fingers should never come within 2 cm of the rim of the glass. The best way in which to make cocktails is to place the glass on a flat, solid surface and then to pour the drink into the glass.

The glass should never be filled to the brim. The drink should come to within about 1 cm of the top of the rim. Any more tends to cause spillage.

You will need copious amounts of ice, which you should either start to make well in advance of any function that you are holding, or else buy ice especially. The type of ice that you use will have an effect on the drinks that you make, with smaller cubes leaving less space for the drink itself. If the cubes are small, you may therefore need to reduce the amount of ice that you put in your glasses.

The professional bar will go one stage further and have a Hamilton Beach blender. This is very similar to a normal electronic mixer, but with only one whisk attached. The drink is given a quick mix with the blender before being poured into the glass.

Set up

The most important requirement is to have space to work in. A cluttered bar becomes untidy and you are more likely to have accidents as a result. Next you need access to water with which to clean your tools as you go along. It is important that these are cleaned between each cocktail when different types of cocktail are being made, otherwise the flavours mingle.

Ideally, you should have a specific bar area for cocktail-making. However, to start with just set aside part of your kitchen or dining room. Remember that cocktail-making, like cooking, is a messy process.

The professional bar

The major differences between the amateur bar and the professional bar are organisation and equipment.

In a professional bar there is a set place for everything, so that you can almost make drinks by touch. There will be an ice-maker and an ice-crusher, along with a bar blender and Hamilton Beach blender. Such equipment is not cheap and when introducing the equipment in each chapter I will give hints to assist you to maintain it.

The other major difference is presentation. Most people will have seen the film *Cocktail,* which features bartenders throwing bottles around, which is referred to in the trade as 'flair'. It is actually quite dangerous, as well as potentially very expensive. To get round this, any bar in which flair is performed will have rubber bounce mats, which reduce the risk of breakage.

Flair is not suitable in a domestic situation. Only perform it when you are sober and within a specifically designated area. Should you wish to try it, then practise with empty bottles that have insulation tape wrapped round them to reduce the risk of breakage and glass splinters. If you feel confident of performing flair in public then only use almost empty bottles. When the bottle is filled above the one-third level, then the liquor is likely to fly out of the bottle as it spins through the air. At the same time, the fuller the bottle, the more liquor is wasted when it is dropped – and it will get dropped sooner or later.

Shooters

Shooters are usually the easiest drinks to make but the fastest to disappear. They require a minimum of time and equipment and practically no advance preparation.

To make the drinks in this section you will need the following equipment:
2 fl oz shot glasses
Pour spouts or jiggers
A spoon or bar spoon.

A pour spout.

The purpose of a shooter is that it is drunk in one go. To layer a drin,k the ingredient is poured over the back of a spoon into the glass. Alternatively, the same effect can be achieved by tipping the glass slightly on its side and pouring the ingredient slowly down the side of it.

A bar spoon.

Tip

The drinks in this section have a strong concentration of alcohol. At a social event you should try to limit everyone to about three of these drinks if you do not want matters to get out of hand.

■ Nuts to you

Glass: 2 fl oz shot glass
Garnish: none

0.5 fl oz Kahlua/Tia Maria

0.5 fl oz Bailey's Irish Cream

0.5 fl oz Frangelico

Method: pour the ingredients into the glass in the order listed. The Kahlua and Bailey's will form layers. The Frangelico should then be poured in very slowly and will mix with the top layer of Bailey's.

Brain damage

Glass: 2 fl oz shot glass
Garnish: none

0.75 fl oz peach Schnapps

0.75 fl oz Bailey's Irish Cream

4 or 5 drops grenadine

Method: pour the Schnapps into the glass and layer the Bailey's Irish Cream on top. Then drip the grenadine into the centre of the drink until a 'brain' forms.

 ET

Glass: 2 fl oz shot glass
Garnish: none

0.5 fl oz Crème de Menthe (green)

0.5 fl oz Bailey's Irish Cream

0.5 fl oz Jack Daniels

Method: pour the ingredients into the glass in the order listed to form layers.

747

Glass: 2 fl oz shot glass
Garnish: none

0.5 fl oz Kahlua/Tia Maria

0.5 fl oz Bailey's Irish Cream

0.5 fl oz amaretto

Method: pour the ingredients into the glass in the order listed to form layers.

 # B52

Glass: 2 fl oz shot glass
Garnish: none

0.5 fl oz Kahlua/Tia Maria

0.5 fl oz Bailey's Irish Cream

0.5 fl oz Grand Marnier

Method: pour the ingredients into the glass in the order listed to form layers.

■ Slippery nipple

Glass: 2 fl oz shot glass
Garnish: none

0.75 fl oz Sambuca

0.75 fl oz Bailey's Irish Cream

Method: pour the ingredients into the glass in the order listed to form layers.

■ Monkey's lunch

Glass: 2 fl oz shot glass
Garnish: none

0.5 fl oz Kahlua/Tia Maria

0.5 fl oz Crème de Bananes

0.5 fl oz Bailey's Irish Cream

Method: pour the ingredients into the glass in the order listed to form layers.

Short drinks

The drinks in this section are slightly longer than shooters, but are just as easy to make. They are better for parties and large groups because they last longer and have a slower effect than shooters.

To make the drinks in this section you will need the following equipment:
Martini (5–6 fl oz glass), rocks (7 fl oz glass) and whisky (8–12 fl oz glass) glasses
Pour spouts or jiggers
A spoon
A chopping board and sharp knife
A cocktail-shaker
Sipping straws (optional)
Plenty of ice.

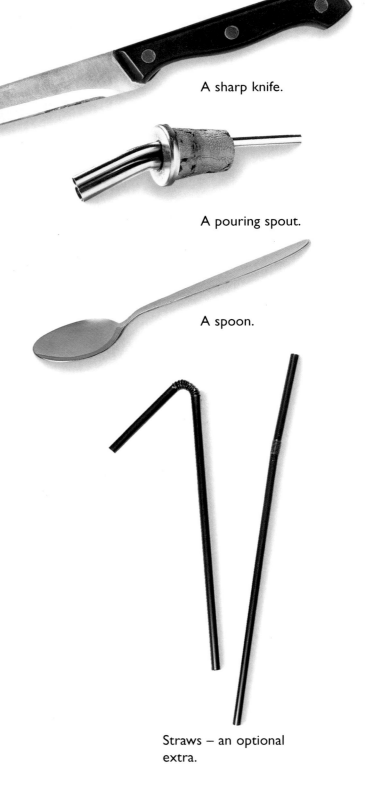

A sharp knife.

A pouring spout.

A spoon.

A cocktail-shaker can be used with or without ice, depending on the recipe. When the drink is to be poured into a chilled glass, it is shaken with ice.

A cocktail-shaker should be used with a short, snappy, shaking motion rather than a rocking motion. When the shaker has ice in it you will know when the drink is ready because the outside of the shaker becomes cold and moisture may begin to appear. Once the drink has been properly mixed, then pour it into the glass immediately.

Proper decorum calls for two sipping straws to be placed in a short cocktail. In reality, these are rarely, if ever, used, and you may feel that they are unnecessary.

Straws – an optional extra.

A dismantled cocktail-shaker.

An ice bucket always looks good on a bar.

A wooden chopping board.

Tips

The easiest way in which to chill a glass is to put ice and soda water into it and then leave it to become cold. Then throw away the ingredients and shake out the excess water before pouring in the drink.

 # Foxhound

Glass: rocks with ice
Garnish: a slice of lemon

2 fl oz brandy

1 measure cranberry juice

1 fl oz Kümmel (German caraway-seed liqueur)

Method: shake the ingredients with ice, then serve.

 **Americano**

Glass: rocks with ice
Garnish: an orange slice

2 fl oz Campari

2 fl oz sweet vermouth

Top up with chilled club soda

Method: stir the Campari and vermouth in an ice-filled tumbler. Add soda to taste.

Bronx

Glass: rocks with ice
Garnish: none

2 fl oz gin

½ fl oz dry vermouth

½ fl oz sweet vermouth

½ fl oz orange juice

Method: add the ingredients to ice cubes and give the whole lot a vigorous shake before straining it into the glass over more ice.

Black Russian

Glass: rocks with ice
Garnish: none

1.5 fl oz vodka

0.75 fl oz Kahlua/Tia Maria

Method: simply pour the ingredients into the glass, passing them over the ice, then stir.

Between the sheets

Glass: chilled Martini glass
Garnish: a lemon twist

0.75 fl oz Cointreau

0.75 fl oz brandy

0.75 fl oz light rum

0.75 fl oz lime juice

Method: shake the ingredients with cracked ice and strain them into a Martini glass. Garnish with the lemon twist.

Variation: should you find the taste too tart, add a small splash of simple syrup before shaking.

Bacardi special

Glass: chilled rocks glass
Garnish: a lime wheel

2 fl oz Bacardi light rum

0.75 fl oz gin

Juice of a small lime

0.5 teaspoon sugar or 1 fl oz simple syrup

Method: shake all the ingredients together (except the rum) with ice. Then add the rum and shake again. Once cold, strain into the glass.

■ Godfather

Glass: rocks with ice
Garnish: none

1.5 fl oz Scotch whisky or bourbon

0.75 fl oz amaretto

Method: simply pour the ingredients into the glass, passing them over the ice, then stir.

■ Creole cocktail

Glass: rocks with ice
Garnish: orange

1 fl oz Malibu

1 fl oz orange juice

1 fl oz vodka

Dash of grenadine

Method: simply pour all the ingredients into a shaker, shake vigorously and pour over ice into the glass.

■ Godmother

Glass: rocks with ice
Garnish: none

1.5 fl oz vodka

0.75 fl oz amaretto

Method: simply pour the ingredients into the glass, passing them over the ice, then stir.

■ Acapulco

Glass: rocks with ice
Garnish: none

1.5 fl oz light rum

1 fl oz Cointreau

3 fl oz pineapple juice

1 fl oz lime juice

Method: shake all the ingredients together with ice, then strain into a glass over ice.

Golden Russian

Glass: rocks with ice
Garnish: none

1.25 fl oz vodka

1 fl oz Galliano

1 fl oz half and half

Method: simply pour the ingredients into the glass, passing them over the ice, then stir.

■ Applejack fizz

Glass: rocks with ice
Garnish: none

3 fl oz Calvados

Juice of half a lemon

1 teaspoon sugar syrup

Method: shake the ingredients with ice, then strain into a glass over ice.

■ Irish nut

Glass: rocks with ice
Garnish: none

1.25 fl oz Frangelico

1 fl oz Bailey's Irish Cream

Method: simply pour the ingredients into the glass, passing them over the ice, then stir.

Rusty nail

Glass: rocks with ice
Garnish: none

1.5 fl oz Scotch whisky

0.75 fl oz Drambuie

Method: simply pour the ingredients into the glass, passing them over the ice, then stir.

■ Sidecar

Glass: chilled Martini glass
Garnish: a lemon slice

1.25 fl oz cognac

0.75 fl oz Cointreau

1 fl oz lemon juice

Method: shake the ingredients with ice and strain into the cocktail glass.

Variation: should you find the taste too tart, add a small splash of simple syrup before shaking.

Toasted almond

Glass: whisky glass with ice
Garnish: none

I fl oz Kahlua/Tia Maria

I fl oz amaretto

I fl oz half and half

Method: simply pour the ingredients into the glass, passing them over the ice, then stir.

■ **White Russian**

Glass: whisky glass with ice
Garnish: none

1.5 fl oz vodka

0.75 fl oz Kahlua/Tia Maria

1 fl oz half and half

Method: pour the vodka and Kahlua into the glass, passing them over the ice, then stir. Once the mixture has settled, slowly pour the half and half on top to form a floating layer.

Long drinks

As their names suggest, the drinks in this section are both longer than short drinks and take longer to drink and digest. I have included some more complicated mixed drinks to get you used to the process of using your cocktail-shaker or mixer.

This section includes some very old and traditional cocktails, most notably the Cuba libre and Moscow mule. You will either love or hate them, as they have very distinctive and unusual tastes. I would therefore advise you to be careful when considering including these drinks on any cocktail list that you present.

To make the drinks in this section you will need the following equipment:
Large highball (12–14 fl oz glass) and wine (10–12 fl oz glass) glasses
Pour spouts or jiggers
A spoon
A chopping board and sharp knife
A cocktail-shaker or Hamilton Beach blender
Thick straws
Plenty of ice.

When the drink is built directly into the glass it may benefit from a stir, either with a spoon or a straw, before serving.

A bar spoon.

A sharp knife.

A teaspoon.

A pour spout.

Measures.

A large highball glass.

Tips

The Hamilton Beach blender is wonderful for mixing drinks. However, it can be improvised by using a hand-held whisk, electric or otherwise, to mix the drink.

Fruit and a chopping board.

Cuba libre

Glass: large highball with ice
Garnish: a lime slice

2 fl oz light rum

1 lime

Coca-cola

Method: pour the rum into a long glass full of ice. Cut the lime in half and squeeze the lime juice into the glass. Drop in one of the lime shells. Top up with Coca-cola and stir.

Wine cup

Glass: large wine glass
Garnish: a cucumber wheel

4 fl oz white wine

4 cubes ice

1 fl oz cassis

0.5 fl oz amaretto

0.5 fl oz cranberry juice

0.5 fl oz pineapple juice

Fill with lemonade

Method: pour the ingredients directly into the glass in the order listed and stir.

■ Mai tai

Glass: wine glass with ice
Garnish: a pineapple slice
and cherry

Method: pour the ingredients directly into the glass in the order listed and stir.

0.75 fl oz light rum

0.75 fl oz dark rum

0.75 fl oz orange Curaçao

0.5 fl oz fresh lime juice

0.5 fl oz grenadine

0.5 fl oz orgeat syrup

0.5 fl oz simple syrup

■ Screwdriver

Glass: Large highball with ice
Garnish: none

1.25 fl oz vodka

3.26 fl oz orange juice

Method: pour the ingredients directly into the glass in the order listed.

■ Moscow mule

Glass: large highball with ice
Garnish: a lime twist and cucumber peel

2 fl oz vodka

Juice of half a lime

Ginger ale

Method: pour the vodka into the glass, followed by the lime juice. Top up with ginger ale and stir.

Sea breeze

Glass: large highball with ice
Garnish: none

1.5 fl oz vodka

1.5 fl oz cranberry juice

1.5 fl oz grapefruit juice

Method: make the drink in the glass, pouring the ingredients in the order listed and adding the juices slowly to form a slight layer.

◼ **Sloe comfortable screw**

Glass: large highball with ice
Garnish: none

1.25 fl oz sloe gin

0.5 fl oz Southern Comfort

0.5 fl oz vodka

3 fl oz orange juice

Method: mix or shake the ingredients together and pour into the glass

■ Sloe comfortable screw up against the wall

Glass: large highball with ice
Garnish: none

1 fl oz sloe gin

0.5 fl oz Southern Comfort

0.5 fl oz vodka

0.5 fl oz Galliano

2.5 fl oz orange juice

Method: mix or shake all the ingredients together except the Galliano. Pour into the glass and float the Galliano on top.

■ Tequila sunrise

Glass: wine glass/large highball with ice
Garnish: an orange slice and speared cherry

1.25 fl oz tequila

3.26 fl oz orange juice

0.27 fl oz grenadine

Method: pour the tequila and orange juice into the glass, then pour the grenadine slowly through the centre of the drink to give a sunrise effect.

Harvey wallbanger

Glass: large highball with ice
Garnish: none

1.25 fl oz vodka

3 fl oz orange juice

0.5 fl oz Galliano

Method: pour the vodka and orange juice into the glass.
Then float the Galliano on top.

■ Pimms special

Glass: wine glass with ice
Garnish: an orange slice and speared cherry

1.25 fl oz Pimms No 1 cup

0.25 fl oz gin

3 fl oz lemonade

Method: pour the ingredients directly into the glass in the order listed.

Variations: reduce the lemonade slightly and add a splash of tonic water, soda or ginger ale.

Hot drinks

These drinks make an ideal conclusion to a meal or a warming influence on a cold evening. Hot drinks provide another, more refined, aspect to cocktail-making. They are made slowly and drunk slowly.

■ 'Monk's' coffee

Glass: heated glass mug

1.75 fl oz Benedictine

2 teaspoons sugar

Hot coffee

Double or heavy whipping cream

Method: stir the liqueur and sugar together, then fill up the glass with coffee to about 1.5 cm short of the rim. Pour the cream slowly onto the top of the drink, possibly using the back of a spoon, to form a layer on top.

■ Liqueur 'Monk's' coffee

Glass: heated glass mug

Pour up to 1.75 fl oz of liqueur (Benedictine) into the bottom of the pre-heated glass cup. Top up the glass to approximately 1.5 cm. from the rim with coffee. The layer of cream is supported by sugar in the coffee. With sweet liqueurs, you will not need to add any sugar to the coffee as this is already contained in the liqueur. Other liqueurs require a small amount of sugar to support the cream layer. Finally, pour whipped or double cream from the back of a spoon onto the top of the drink to form a layer.

■ Hotshot 'Monk's' coffee

Glass: heated 2 fl oz shot glass

0.75 fl oz Benedictine

1 teaspoon sugar

0.75 fl oz hot coffee

Double or heavy whipping cream

Method: stir the liqueur and sugar together, then add the coffee. Finally, float the cream on top of the drink.

■ 'Normandy' coffee

Glass: heated glass mug

1.75 fl oz Calvados

2 teaspoons sugar

Hot coffee

Double or heavy whipping cream

Method: stir the liqueur and sugar together, then fill up the glass with coffee to about 1.5 cm short of the rim. Pour the cream slowly onto the top of the drink, possibly using the back of a spoon, to form a layer on top.

■ Liqueur 'Normandy' coffee

Glass: heated glass mug

Pour up to 1.75 fl oz of liqueur into the bottom of the pre-heated glass cup. Top up the glass to approximately 1.5 cm. from the rim with coffee. The layer of cream is supported by sugar in the coffee. With sweet liqueurs you will not need to add any sugar to the coffee as this is already contained in the liqueur. Other liqueurs require a small amount of sugar to support the cream layer. Finally, pour whipped or double cream from the back of a spoon onto the top of the drink to form a layer.

■ Hotshot 'Normandy' coffee

Glass: heated 2 fl oz shot glass

0.75 fl oz Calvados

1 teaspoon sugar

0.75 fl oz hot coffee

Double or heavy whipping cream

Method: stir the liqueur and sugar together, then add the coffee. Finally, float the cream on top of the drink.

■ 'Mexican' coffee

Glass: heated glass mug

1.75 fl oz Kahlua

2 teaspoons sugar

Hot coffee

Double or heavy whipping cream

Method: stir the liqueur and sugar together, then fill up the glass with coffee to about 1.5 cm short of the rim. Pour the cream slowly onto the top of the drink, possibly using the back of a spoon, to form a layer on top.

■ Hotshot 'Mexican' coffee

Glass: heated 2 fl oz shot glass

0.75 fl oz Kahlua

1 teaspoon sugar

0.75 fl oz hot coffee

Double or heavy whipping cream

Method: stir the liqueur and sugar together, then add the coffee. Finally, float the cream on top of the drink.

■ 'French' coffee

Glass: heated glass mug

1.75 fl oz brandy

2 teaspoons sugar

Hot coffee

Double or heavy whipping cream

Method: stir the liqueur and sugar together, then fill up the glass with coffee to about 1.5 cm short of the rim. Pour the cream slowly onto the top of the drink, possibly using the back of a spoon, to form a layer on top.

■ Hotshot 'French' coffee

Glass: heated 2 fl oz shot glass

0.75 fl oz brandy

1 teaspoon sugar

0.75 fl oz hot coffee

Double or heavy whipping cream

Method: stir the liqueur and sugar together, then add the coffee. Finally, float the cream on top of the drink.

■ Liqueur 'French' coffee

Glass: heated glass mug

Pour up to 1.75 fl oz of liqueur (brandy) into the bottom of the pre-heated glass cup. Top up the glass to approximately 1.5 cm. from the rim with coffee. The layer of cream is supported by sugar in the coffee. With sweet liqueurs, you will not need to add any sugar to the coffee as this is already contained in the liqueur. Other liqueurs require a small amount of sugar to support the cream layer. Finally, pour whipped or double cream from the back of a spoon onto the top of the drink to form a layer.

■ 'Prince Charles' coffee

Glass: heated glass mug

1.75 fl oz Drambuie

2 teaspoons sugar

Hot coffee

Double or heavy whipping cream

Method: stir the liqueur and sugar together, then fill up the glass with coffee to about 1.5 cm short of the rim. Pour the cream slowly onto the top of the drink, possibly using the back of a spoon, to form a layer on top.

■ 'Irish' hotshot

Glass: heated 2 fl oz shot glass

0.75 fl oz Irish whiskey

1 teaspoon sugar

0.75 fl oz hot coffee

Double or heavy whipping cream

Method: stir the liqueur and sugar together, then add the coffee. Finally, float the cream on top of the drink.

■ 'Caribbean' coffee

Glass: heated glass mug

1.75 fl oz rum

2 teaspoons sugar

Hot coffee

Double or heavy whipping cream

Method: stir the liqueur and sugar together, then fill up the glass with coffee to about 1.5 cm short of the rim. Pour the cream slowly onto the top of the drink, possibly using the back of a spoon, to form a layer on top.

'Scottish' hotshot

Glass: heated 2 fl oz shot glass

0.75 fl oz Scotch whisky

1 teaspoon sugar

0.75 fl oz hot coffee

Double or heavy whipping cream

Method: stir the liqueur and sugar together, then add the coffee. Finally, float the cream on top of the drink.

'Scottish' coffee

Glass: heated glass mug

1.75 fl oz Scotch whisky

2 teaspoons sugar

Hot coffee

Double or heavy whipping cream

Method: stir the liqueur and sugar together, then fill up the glass with coffee to about 1.5 cm short of the rim. Pour the cream slowly onto the top of the drink, possibly using the back of a spoon, to form a layer on top.

■ Hot chocolate

Glass: warmed glass mug

Packet of hot-chocolate mix

Hot water or milk (as per instructions on packet)

Chocolate chips

Method: add the mix to the water or milk and stir vigorously. Pour into the mug and top with the chocolate chips. Finish off by shaking the remains of the mix from the packet onto the top of the chocolate chips.

■ 'Almond' chocolate

Glass: warmed glass mug

1.75 fl oz amaretto

Packet of hot-chocolate mix

Hot water or milk (as per instructions on packet)

Aerosol cream or mini-marshmallows

Method: add the mix to the water or milk and stir vigorously. Pour the liqueur into the mug, followed by the mix. Top with the marshmallows or aerosol cream. Finish off by shaking the remains of the mix from the packet onto the top of the cream or marshmallows.

Chocolate sundae

Glass: warmed glass mug

1.75 fl oz banana liqueur

Packet of hot-chocolate mix

Hot water or milk (as per instructions on packet)

Cream

Method: add the mix to the water or milk and stir vigorously. Pour the liqueur into the mug, followed by the mix. Top with the cream, poured on over a spoon.

Hotchoc sundae

Glass: heated 2 fl oz shot glass

0.75 fl oz banana liqueur

0.75 fl oz hot chocolate

Cream

Method: pour the liqueur into the glass, then pour in the hot chocolate. Stir together. Finally, float the cream on top of the drink.

■ Chocolate orange

Glass: warmed glass mug

1.75 fl oz Cointreau

Packet of hot-chocolate mix

Hot water or milk (as per instructions on packet)

Aerosol cream or mini-marshmallows

Method: add the mix to the water or milk and stir vigorously. Pour the liqueur into the mug, followed by the mix. Top with the marshmallows or aerosol cream. Finish off by shaking the remains of the mix from the packet onto the top of the cream or marshmallows.

■ Hotchoc orange

Glass: heated 2 fl oz shot glass

0.75 fl oz Cointreau

0.75 fl oz hot chocolate

Double or heavy whipping cream

Method: pour the liqueur into the glass, then pour in the hot chocolate. Stir together. Finally, float the cream on top of the drink.

■ 'Strawberry' chocolate

Glass: warmed glass mug

1.75 fl oz Fraise liqueur

Packet of hot-chocolate mix

Hot water or milk (as per instructions on packet)

Aerosol cream or mini-marshmallows

Method: add the mix to the water or milk and stir vigorously. Pour the liqueur into the mug, followed by the mix. Top with the marshmallows or aerosol cream. Finish off by shaking the remains of the mix from the packet onto the top of the cream or marshmallows.

■ 'Strawberry' hotchoc

Glass: heated 2 fl oz shot glass

0.75 fl oz Fraise liqueur

0.75 fl oz hot chocolate

Double or heavy whipping cream

Method: pour the liqueur into the glass, then pour in the hot chocolate. Stir together. Finally, float the cream on top of the drink.

■ 'Calypso' chocolate

Glass: heated glass mug

1.75 fl oz Tia Maria

2 teaspoons sugar

Hot chocolate

Double or heavy whipping cream

Method: stir the liqueur and sugar together, then fill up the glass with hot chocolate to about 1.5 cm short of the rim. Pour the cream slowly onto the top of the drink, possibly using the back of a spoon, to form a layer on top.

■ 'Calypso' hotshot

Glass: heated 2 fl oz shot glass

0.75 fl oz Tia Maria

1 teaspoon sugar

0.75 fl oz hot coffee

Double or heavy whipping cream

Method: stir the liqueur and sugar together, then add the coffee. Finally, float the cream on top of the drink.

■ 'Cherry' hotchoc

Glass: heated 2 fl oz shot glass

0.75 fl oz Kirsch

0.75 fl oz hot chocolate

Double or heavy whipping cream

Method: pour the liqueur into the glass, then pour in the hot chocolate. Stir together. Finally, float the cream on top of the drink.

'Coconut' chocolate

Glass: warmed glass mug

1.75 fl oz Malibu

Packet of hot-chocolate mix

Hot water or milk (as per instructions on packet)

Aerosol cream or mini-marshmallows

Method: add the mix to the water or milk and stir vigorously. Pour the liqueur into the mug, followed by the mix. Top with the marshmallows or aerosol cream. Finish off by shaking the remains of the mix from the packet onto the top of the cream or marshmallows.

'Coconut' hotchoc

Glass: heated 2 fl oz shot glass

0.75 fl oz Malibu

0.75 fl oz hot chocolate

Double or heavy whipping cream

Method: pour the liqueur into the glass, then pour in the hot chocolate. Stir together. Finally, float the cream on top of the drink.

Fruit-based drinks

Party time! By now you should have mastered the basics, so we will start to expand your knowledge. Once you have dealt with this chapter you should be competent enough to hold parties of your own.

This section includes some very old and traditional cocktails. You will either love or hate these drinks, as they have very distinctive and unusual tastes. I would therefore advise that you carefully consider including them on any cocktail list that you present.

To make the drinks in this section you will need the following equipment:
Large highball (12–14 fl oz glass) and wine (10–12 fl oz glass) glasses
Pour spouts or jiggers
A spoon
A chopping board and sharp knife
A cocktail-shaker or a Hamilton Beach blender
Thick straws
Plenty of ice
Measuring cups.

When the drink is built directly into the glass it may benefit from a stir, either with a spoon or a straw, before serving.

A large highball glass.

Measuring cups.

A spoon.

A sharp knife.

A pouring spout.

A cocktail-shaker.

Tips
The Hamilton Beach blender is wonderful for mixing drinks. However, it can be improvised by using a hand-held whisk, electric or otherwise, to mix the drink.

■ Killer zombie

Glass: large highball with ice
Garnish: an orange slice/cherry

0.5 fl oz light rum

0.5 fl oz dark rum

0.5 fl oz apricot brandy

0.5 fl oz triple sec

1.25 fl oz pineapple juice

1.25 fl oz orange juice

Method: mix or shake the ingredients together and pour them into the glass.

■ Cobra's venom

Glass: large highball with ice
Garnish: an orange squeeze

0.5 fl oz gin

0.5 fl oz vodka

0.5 fl oz brandy

0.5 fl oz blue Curaçao

3.5 fl oz orange juice

Method: mix or shake the ingredients together and pour them into the glass.

■ Bloody Mary

Glass: large highball with ice
Garnish: a lime squeeze, celery stick

1.25 fl oz vodka

4 fl oz Bloody Mary mix (see below)

Method: build the drink straight into the glass.

Basic Bloody Mary mix
3.5 fl oz tomato juice
0.25 fl oz lemon juice
2 dashes Worcestershire sauce
2 drops Tabasco
Salt and pepper to taste

■ Margarita

Glass: chilled Martini glass
Garnish: salt rim

1.25 fl oz tequila

1 fl oz triple sec

1 fl oz freshly squeezed lime juice

Method: shake the ingredients in a cocktail-shaker with ice, strain and pour them into the glass.

June bug

Glass: large highball with ice
Garnish: none

1.25 fl oz Midori

0.5 fl oz Malibu

0.5 fl oz banana liqueur

2 fl oz pineapple juice

Juice of 1 lemon

Dash of simple syrup

Method: mix or shake the ingredients together and pour them into the glass.

Fire-eater

Glass: large highball with ice
Garnish: an orange wheel/lime squeeze

1 fl oz tequila

1 fl oz triple sec

2 fl oz orange juice

1.25 fl oz cranberry juice

Method: pour all the ingredients in the glass in the order listed. The cranberry juice should float at the top of the drink.

◼ Zombie

Glass: large highball with ice
Garnish: a pineapple slice/cherry

1 fl oz light rum

0.5 fl oz dark rum

0.5 fl oz triple sec

1.25 fl oz pineapple juice

1.25 fl oz passionfruit juice

0.5 fl oz lemon juice

Method: mix or shake the ingredients together and pour them into the glass.
Variation: add a dash of simple syrup.

◼ Monkey's lunch 2

Glass: large highball with ice
Garnish: a pineapple slice/cherry

1 fl oz banana liqueur

0.75 fl oz light rum

0.5 fl oz white Crème de Cacao

1.5 fl oz pineapple juice

1.5 fl oz cranberry juice

Method: mix or shake the ingredients together and pour them into the glass.

◼ Peach on the beach

Glass: large highball with ice
Garnish: a peach slice

1.25 fl oz vodka

0.75 fl oz peach Schnapps

1.5 fl oz orange juice

1.5 fl oz cranberry juice

Method: mix or shake the ingredients together and pour them into the glass.

◼ Planter's punch

Glass: large highball with ice
Garnish: a pineapple slice/cherry

1.25 fl oz white rum

Juice of 1 lime

Dash of grenadine

2 dashes angostura bitters

3 fl oz orange juice

Method: mix or shake the ingredients together and pour them into the glass.

■ Fuzzy navel

Glass: large highball with ice
Garnish: none

2 fl oz peach Schnapps

3 fl oz orange juice

Method: pour the ingredients into the glass and stir.

■ The joker

Glass: large highball with ice
Garnish: an orange squeeze

0.75 fl oz peach Schnapps

0.75 fl oz Malibu

0.75 fl oz blue Curaçao

3 fl oz orange juice

Method: mix or shake the ingredients together and pour them into the glass.

◼ Sex on the beach

Glass: large highball with ice
Garnish: none

0.5 fl oz Southern Comfort

0.5 fl oz amaretto

0.5 fl oz vodka

0.5 fl oz dark rum

1.5 fl oz pineapple juice

1.5 fl oz orange juice

Dash of grenadine

Method: build up the ingredients directly into the glass.

◼ Yellowbird

Glass: large highball with ice
Garnish: an orange slice

1.25 fl oz light rum

0.5 fl oz Galliano

0.5 fl oz banana liqueur

1.5 fl oz pineapple juice

1.5 fl oz orange juice

Method: mix or shake the ingredients together and pour them into the glass.

Iced teas

■ Boston

Glass: large highball with ice
Garnish: a lemon slice

0.5 fl oz gin

0.5 fl oz light rum

0.6 fl oz Kahlua/Tia Maria

0.5 fl oz vodka

0.5 fl oz lemon juice

Dash of simple syrup

Top with Coca-cola

Method: mix or shake all of the ingredients together except for the Coca-cola. Pour into the glass and top with Coca-cola.

Long beach

Glass: large highball with ice
Garnish: a lemon slice

0.5 fl oz gin

0.5 fl oz light rum

0.5 fl oz triple sec

0.5 fl oz vodka

0.5 fl oz lemon juice

Dash of simple syrup

Top with cranberry juice

Method: mix or shake the ingredients together except for the cranberry juice. Pour into the glass and top with the cranberry juice.

Long Island

Glass: large highball with ice
Garnish: a lemon slice

0.5 fl oz gin

0.5 fl oz light rum

0.5 fl oz triple sec

0.5 fl oz vodka

0.5 fl oz lemon juice

Dash of simple syrup

Top with Coca-cola

Method: mix or shake all of the ingredients together except for the Coca-cola. Pour into the glass and top with Coca-cola.

 # Texan

Glass: large highball with ice
Garnish: a lemon squeeze

0.5fl oz light rum

0.5 fl oz tequila

0.5 fl oz triple sec

0.5 fl oz vodka

0.5 fl oz lemon juice

Dash of simple syrup

Top with Coca-cola

Method: mix or shake all of the ingredients together except for the Coca-cola. Pour into the glass and top with Coca-cola.

Ultimate

Glass: large highball with ice
Garnish: a lemon squeeze

0.5 fl oz gin

0.5 fl oz light rum

0.5 fl oz tequila

0.5 fl oz triple sec

0.5 fl oz vodka

0.5 fl oz lemon juice

Dash of simple syrup/Top with Coca-cola

Method: mix or shake all of the ingredients together except for the Coca-cola. Pour into the glass and top with Coca-cola.

Cream-based drinks

Best as a 'first' drink to line the stomach or as a light substitute for dessert, these drinks are easy on the stomach and palate.

■ Grasshopper

Glass: large highball with ice
Garnish: none

1.25 fl oz green Crème de Menthe

1 fl oz white Crème de Cacao

3 fl oz half and half

Method: mix or shake the ingredients together and pour them into the glass.

■ Banana banshee

Glass: large highball with ice
Garnish: none

1 fl oz Crème de Cacao

1 fl oz banana liqueur

3 fl oz half and half

Method: mix or shake the ingredients together and pour them into the glass.

■ Pina colada

Glass: large highball with ice
Garnish: a pineapple slice/cherry

1.25 fl oz light rum

4 fl oz Pina-colada mix (see below)

Method: mix or shake the ingredients together and pour them into the glass.

Basic Pina-colada mix
3 fl oz pineapple juice
1 fl oz coconut cream

Variation: add any or all of the following and blend them together to make a smooth mix for parties:
a) pineapple rings
b) orange juice or half and half.

■ Brandy Alexander

Glass: Martini glass
Garnish: a sprinkle of nutmeg

1 fl oz brandy

1 fl oz Crème de Cacao

1 fl oz half and half

Method: shake the ingredients with ice and pour them into the glass.

Tips
Pina-colada mix and half and half will keep for about two to three days, but, as with everything else, are best served fresh. Store them in the fridge when not in use.

■ Aggravation

Glass: large highball with ice
Garnish: none

1 fl oz whisky

1 fl oz Kahlua/Tia Maria

3.25 fl oz half and half

Method: mix or shake the ingredients together and pour them into the glass.

■ Banana nut 2

Glass: large highball with ice
Garnish: none

1.25 fl oz banana liqueur

1 fl oz Frangelico

3 fl oz half and half

Method: mix or shake the ingredients together and pour them into the glass.

Advanced drinks

Ice-cream drinks are best served either on their own or at the end of a meal as a substitute for dessert. They take practice to get right, but once you have got the hang of them, making all other frozen drinks will become relatively simple.

To make the drinks in this section you will need the following equipment:
Wine (10–12 fl oz) glasses
Pour spouts or jiggers
A blender
A crushed-ice-maker (optional)
An ice-cream scoop
A small ice scoop (4 ins to 4½ins)
Large straws
Plenty of ice
A sharp knife and chopping board.

When selecting a bar blender you should consider purchasing a blender which will blend whole ice. This type of blender will be more durable and will therefore last longer.

When using a blender, always put the liquid ingredients in first. If you put the ice cream, ice or sorbet in first they can clog the blades. While the drink is blending, air pockets may form, preventing the proper circulation of the contents. If this happens, switch off the blender, allow the contents to settle, encouraging this by tapping the base or side of the blender against your hand. Never tap it against a hard surface as you are likely to break the blender.

When you are blending a drink, always start with the lowest speed. A faster blender will produce the drink more quickly but is more likely to make the drink runny. Blended drinks should have enough consistency to support a straw standing in the centre. When using the blender, you should see a line appear across the drink when it is ready. If you can see down to the blades it is too runny. If this happens, then you should add crushed ice and blend for slightly longer. It

Tip

For the recipes in this part of the book you will need a blender. A household blender will be sufficient to start with, but you will need a proper bar blender for making more than a small number of these drinks. This will be the most expensive piece of equipment in any domestic bar except for a fridge.

is important that the right amount of ice is added the first time. Every time you stop the blender and start again you will allow the ice cream to melt further. Therefore, start off by putting at least half a scoop of crushed ice in the drink or, if you have a lid with a hole in it, insert crushed ice through the top of the blender.

When making blended drinks, always use crushed ice. The blender will then last longer. At the same time you should always ensure that the gears of the blender are properly joined before switching it on and that the blades have stopped rotating before it is taken off the base.

Crushed ice is best produced by using a crushed-ice-maker. However, if you do not have one, place your ice in a tea towel on a solid chopping board or hard surface and attack it with a hammer or rolling pin to break up the ice. This will reduce the wear on the blender and make it easier to blend the drink.

When the drink is ready, it may need some encouragement to pour out of the blender cup. If so, then tap it against your hand whilst pouring, but be careful not to get too close to the glass. If you really want to show off, then put the straw in the drink in the blender cup. When the drink pours out, the straw should come out with it and end up standing in the drink.

You should not use 'soft-scoop' ice cream as the drink will not become the proper consistency. Standard vanilla ice cream is the best to use, although French vanilla ice cream gives a good taste.

Most cream-based cocktails can be turned into frozen cocktails by adjusting the recipes slightly and blending them with ice cream. An ice-cream cocktail will usually only contain about 1.5 fl oz of alcohol and the measurements should therefore be adjusted accordingly.

■ Banana banshee (screaming)

Glass: wine glass
Garnish: a banana slice

Half a ripe banana

0.5 fl oz Crème de Cacao

0.5 fl oz banana liqueur

0.5 fl oz vodka

0.5 fl oz half and half

Method: place the ingredients in the blender in the order listed and blend until smooth.

■ Banana coffee

Glass: wine glass
Garnish: a banana slice

Half a ripe banana

1.25 fl oz banana liqueur

1 fl oz Kahlua/Tia Maria

2.5 scoops vanilla ice cream

Method: place the ingredients in the blender in the order listed and blend until smooth.

■ Banana chocolate

Glass: wine glass
Garnish: a banana slice

Half a ripe banana

1.25 fl oz banana liqueur

1 fl oz chocolate syrup

2.5 scoops of vanilla ice cream

Method: place the ingredients in the blender in the order listed and blend until smooth.

■ Banana nut

Glass: wine glass
Garnish: a banana slice/nutmeg

Half a ripe banana

1.25 fl oz Frangelico

1 fl oz banana liqueur

2.5 scoops of vanilla ice cream

Method: place the ingredients in the blender in the order listed and blend until smooth. Sprinkle a small amount of nutmeg over the drink before serving.

■ Chocolate mint

Glass: wine glass
Garnish: none

1 fl oz peppermint Schnapps

1 fl oz white Crème de Cacao

1 fl oz chocolate syrup

2.5 scoops of vanilla ice cream

Method: place the ingredients in the blender in the order listed and blend until smooth.

■ Chocolate strawberry

Glass: wine glass
Garnish: a strawberry

3 fresh strawberries

1.25 fl oz Fraise liqueur

1 fl oz Kahlua

1 fl oz chocolate syrup

2.5 scoops of vanilla ice cream

Method: place the ingredients in the blender in the order listed and blend until smooth.

■ Golden Cadillac

Glass: wine glass
Garnish: none

1.25 fl oz Galliano

1 fl oz white Crème de Cacao

0.75 fl oz half and half

2.5 scoops of vanilla ice cream

Method: place the ingredients in the blender in the order listed and blend until smooth.

■ Grasshopper

Glass: wine glass
Garnish: none

1.25 fl oz green Crème de Menthe

1 fl oz white Crème de Cacao

0.75 fl oz half and half

2.5 scoops of vanilla ice cream

Method: place the ingredients in the blender in the order listed and blend until smooth.

■ Irish banana

Glass: wine glass
Garnish: a banana slice

Half a ripe banana

1.25 fl oz banana liqueur

1 fl oz Bailey's Irish Cream

Method: place the ingredients in the blender in the order listed and blend until smooth.

■ Sloe comfort

Glass: wine glass
Garnish: a strawberry

1.25 fl oz sloe gin

1 fl oz Southern Comfort

0.5 fl oz grenadine

2.5 scoops of vanilla ice cream

Method: place the ingredients in the blender in the order listed and blend until smooth.

Frozen-sorbet drinks

Sorbet drinks are an extension of standard frozen drinks. It is more difficult to get the right consistency, however, due to the nature of sorbet. Most fruit-juice drinks can be turned into sorbet cocktails by the use of an appropriately flavoured sorbet and a reduction in the quantities of the other ingredients.

To make the drinks in this section you will need the following equipment:
Wine glasses (10–12 fl oz)
Pour spouts or jiggers
A blender
A crushed-ice-maker (optional)
An ice-cream scoop
A small ice scoop (4 ins to 4½ins)
Large straws
Plenty of ice
A sharp knife and chopping board.

Should you wish to serve a sorbet drink as a dessert, then I suggest that you top off the drink with whipped cream (preferably from an aerosol) and a cherry. To apply aerosol cream, you should spray on the cream in circles from the outside of the drink inwards, forming a cone of cream.

Tip
Sorbet does not generally provide as good a consistency as ice cream. It is therefore more likely that you will need to add crushed ice and you should also make sure that you use the sorbet straight out of the freezer.

▪ Bahama frost

Glass: wine glass
Garnish: a pineapple slice/cherry

0.5 fl oz Midori

0.5 fl oz Malibu

0.5 fl oz banana liqueur

2.5 scoops of orange sorbet

Method: place the ingredients in the blender in the order listed and blend until smooth.

▪ Frozen screwdriver

Glass: wine glass
Garnish: aerosol whipping cream

1.2 fl oz vodka

0.5 fl oz orange juice

2.5 scoops of orange sorbet

Method: place the ingredients in the blender in the order listed and blend until smooth.

■ Frozen hurricane

Glass: wine glass
Garnish: none

1.25 fl oz light rum

0.5 fl oz grenadine

2.5 scoops of lemon sorbet

Method: place the ingredients in the blender in the order listed and blend until smooth.

■ Green eyes

Glass: wine glass
Garnish: a lime wheel

0.5 fl oz vodka

0.5 fl oz blue Curaçao

0.5 fl oz orange juice

2.5 scoops orange sorbet

Method: place the ingredients in the blender in the order listed and blend until smooth.

Frozen-ice drinks

This is the standard type of frozen drink and practically any cocktail can be turned into a frozen drink with the appliance of crushed ice and a blender. However, this will not necessarily produce the best variation of the cocktail, and you should therefore consider whether it would be more appropriate to make ice-cream or sorbet cocktails wherever possible.

To make the drinks in this section you will need the following equipment:
Wine glasses (10–12 fl oz)
Pour spouts or jiggers
A blender
A crushed-ice-maker (optional)
A small ice scoop
Large straws
Plenty of ice
A sharp knife and chopping board
A 'rim' set-up.

Tip
As you are using crushed ice, the drink will blend much faster and will also deteriorate much more quickly. You should therefore pay careful attention when blending and switch off the blender as soon as the drink is done. The drink should then be served as soon as possible before it starts to melt.

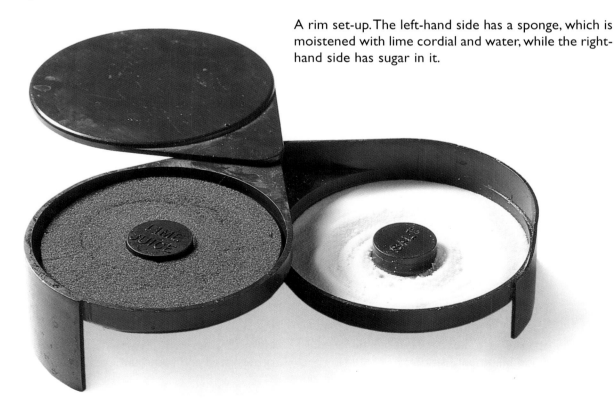

A rim set-up. The left-hand side has a sponge, which is moistened with lime cordial and water, while the right-hand side has sugar in it.

■ Apricot daquiri

Glass: wine glass
Garnish: an apricot slice

Quarter of a small apricot

1 fl oz light rum

0.75 fl oz apricot liqueur

0.5 fl oz lime juice

1 teaspoon sugar

1 scoop of crushed ice

Method: place the ingredients in the blender in the order listed and blend until smooth.

■ Banana daquiri

Glass: wine glass
Garnish: a banana slice

Half a ripe banana

1 fl oz light rum

0.75 fl oz banana liqueur

0.5 fl oz lime juice

1 teaspoon sugar

1 scoop of crushed ice

Method: place the ingredients in the blender in the order listed and blend until smooth.

■ Chee-chee

Glass: wine glass
Garnish: a pineapple slice/cherry

1.25 fl oz vodka

4 fl oz Pina-colada mix (see below)

1 scoop of crushed ice

Method: place the ingredients in the blender in the order listed and blend until smooth.

Basic Pina-colada mix
3 fl oz pineapple juice
1 fl oz coconut cream

■ Lime daquiri

Glass: wine glass
Garnish: a lime wheel

1.25 fl oz light rum

1 fl oz lime juice

1 fl oz simple syrup

1 scoop of crushed ice

Method: place the ingredients in the blender in the order listed and blend until smooth.

Lime margarita

Glass: wine glass with salt rim
Garnish: a lime wheel

1.25 fl oz tequila

0.75 fl oz triple sec

1 fl oz fresh lime juice

1 scoop of crushed ice

Method: place the ingredients in the blender in the order listed and blend until smooth.

Peach fuzz

Glass: wine glass
Garnish: a peach slice

3 peach slices (canned)

1 fl oz vodka

1 fl oz peach Schnapps

1 fl oz half and half

1 scoop of crushed ice

Method: place the ingredients in the blender in the order listed and blend until smooth.

■ Peach margarita

Glass: wine glass with sugar rim
Garnish: a lime wheel

3 peach slices (canned)

1.25 fl oz tequila

0.5 fl oz peach Schnapps

1 fl oz fresh lime juice

1 scoop of crushed ice

Method: place the ingredients in the blender in the order listed and blend until smooth.

■ Pina colada

Glass: wine glass
Garnish: a pineapple slice and cherry

1.25 fl oz light rum

4 fl oz Pina-colada mix (see below)

1 scoop of crushed ice

Method: place the ingredients in the blender in the order listed and blend until smooth.

Basic Pina-colada mix
3 fl oz pineapple juice
1 fl oz coconut cream

■ Strawberry daquiri

Glass: wine glass
Garnish: a strawberry

4 fresh strawberries

1.25 fl oz light rum

0.75 fl oz strawberry liqueur

0.5 fl oz lime juice

1 teaspoon sugar

1 scoop of crushed ice

Method: place the ingredients in the blender in the order listed and blend until smooth.

■ Strawberry margarita

Glass: wine glass with sugar rim
Garnish: a lime wheel and strawberry

4 fresh strawberries

1.25 fl oz tequila

0.75 fl oz triple sec

1 fl oz fresh lime juice

1 scoop of crushed ice

Method: place the ingredients in the blender in the order listed and blend until smooth.

Old style

**In this section I've included some
'classic' old cocktails.**

All of the cocktails in this section are simple to make and require no further explanation.

To make the drinks in this section you will need the following equipment:
Glass mug, Martini (5–6 fl oz) glass, whisky (8–12 fl oz) glass, champagne flute (8–10 fl oz), wine (10–12 fl oz) glass and large highball glasses (12–14 fl oz)
Pour spouts or jiggers
Large straws
Plenty of ice
A sharp knife and chopping board.

 ## Collins

Glass: large highball with ice
Garnish: a lemon squeeze

2 fl oz liqueur*

Juice of 1 lemon

1 fl oz simple syrup

Top with soda water

Method: pour all the ingredients except the soda water into the glass, stir and then top with the soda water.

*The variations of liqueurs in Collins are as follows:

Jack	apple brandy
John	gin (Europe)
	bourbon (North America)
Mike	Irish whiskey
Pedro	rum
Pierre	cognac
Tom	vodka (Europe)
	gin (North America).

■ **Bellini**

Glass: champagne flute
Garnish: none

Peach juice

Champagne

Method: fill the glass approximately one-third full of peach juice and top it up with champagne.

Alternatives: instead of using peach nectar you could purée peaches in a blender with some added sugar.

■ Gibson

Glass: chilled Martini glass
Garnish: two cocktail onions

A dry Martini decorated with two cocktail onions –
for the recipe, see Martini below.

Martini

Glass: chilled Martini glass
Garnish: a lemon twist or olive

2 fl oz gin or vodka

Dash of vermouth

Method: this cocktail may be served in a number of
ways. Shaking is accused of 'bruising' the drink and
does produce a slightly different taste. Stirring is
supposed to retain the whole flavour. Alternatively, the
drink may be served on the rocks, using a whisky glass
and stirring the drink in the glass. It is essential that
the drink is served cold for the best taste.

■ Gimlet

Glass: wine glass with ice
Garnish: a lime squeeze

2 fl oz gin or vodka

1 fl oz Rose's lime juice

Method: build the drink up straight into the glass

■ Gin fizz

Glass: chilled whisky glass
Garnish: none

2 fl oz gin

1 fl oz lemon juice

1 fl oz simple syrup

Top with soda water

Method: shake all the ingredients except for the soda water vigorously with ice. Strain into the glass and immediately top up with soda water. The drink should be drunk before the fizzing stops.

Variations:
a) Alabama – add two mint sprigs
b) Texan – add 0.5 fl oz orange juice and 0.5 fl oz lemon juice
c) silver – add an egg white.

■ Gin rickey

Glass: large highball with ice
Garnish: a lime twist

2 fl oz gin

1 fl oz lime juice

2 dashes of grenadine

Top with soda water

Method: pour the ingredients directly into the glass in the order listed, stirring before topping with the soda water.

■ Gin sling

Glass: large highball with ice
Garnish: an orange slice

2 fl oz gin

1 fl oz cherry brandy

1 fl oz lemon juice

Top with soda water

Method: pour the ingredients directly into the glass in the order listed, stirring before topping with the soda water.

■ Kir

Glass: wine glass
Garnish: none

0.5 fl oz Crème de Cassis

6 fl oz dry white wine

Method: pour the ingredients into the glass in the order listed.

Kir royale

Glass: champagne flute
Garnish: none

0.5 fl oz Crème de Cassis

6 fl oz champagne

Method: pour the ingredients into the glass in the order listed.

Mint julep

Glass: whisky glass
Garnish: mint leaves

2 fl oz bourbon

0.5 fl oz simple syrup

1 dozen fresh mint leaves

Method: place 1 fl oz of bourbon and 10 mint leaves into the glass. Muddle the ingredients together with a pestle (or the back of a spoon). Add crushed ice to fill the glass half full and stir. Add the rest of the bourbon, stir again and garnish with the remaining mint leaves.

◼ Mulled wine

Glass: heated mug
Garnish: a lemon and cloves

6 fl oz red wine

6 fl oz port

10 fl oz brandy

0.5 pint water

1 medium-sized cinnamon stick

2 lemons

4 cloves

0.5 tablespoon brown sugar

Method: cut the lemons in half and push the cloves into the skins. Place the ingredients in a suitably sized saucepan. Heat through thoroughly, but do not allow the mixture to boil. Serve in heated mugs.

◼ Old-fashioned

Glass: whisky glass
Garnish: an orange slice and cherry

2 fl oz bourbon

2 dashes of angostura bitters

0.5 fl oz simple syrup

Method: mix the angostura bitters and syrup with a dash of bourbon. Fill the glass two-thirds full with ice cubes and add the rest of the bourbon. Top up with ice. Squeeze the orange slice into the glass and drop it into the drink along with the cherry.

■ Orange fizz

Glass: chilled whisky glass
Garnish: none

1.25 fl oz gin

0.5 fl oz triple sec

1 fl oz lemon juice

1 fl oz orange juice

1 fl oz simple syrup

Top with soda water

Method: shake all the ingredients except for the soda water vigorously with ice. Strain into the glass and immediately top up with soda water. The drink should be drunk before the fizzing stops.

■ Whisky sour

Glass: large highball with ice
Garnish: an orange slice

2 fl oz bourbon

0.5 fl oz lemon juice

0.5 fl oz simple syrup

Method: mix or shake the ingredients together and pour into the glass.

Non-alcoholic drinks

These drinks are included to provide easy options for the designated driver or children. However, you should be able to reproduce most cocktails in a non-alcoholic form.

To make the drinks in this section you will need the following equipment:
Large highball glasses (12–14 fl oz)
Pour spouts or jiggers
A blender
A cocktail-shaker or mixer
Large straws
Plenty of ice
A sharp knife and chopping board.

Straws.

Tip: milk shakes
Milk shakes are among the easiest drinks to make. The basic constituents remain the same, namely milk and three scoops of vanilla ice cream. To help the ice cream blend properly, you need approximately 3 fl oz of liquid. This is made up of milk and whatever flavour of ingredients that you choose to add.

A blender.

 **Banana**

Glass: large highball
Garnish: none

Three-quarters of a ripe banana

2 fl oz milk

3 scoops of vanilla ice cream

Method: blend the ingredients together until smooth.

Banana-strawberry

Glass: large highball
Garnish: none

Half a ripe banana

3 fresh strawberries

2 fl oz milk

3 scoops of vanilla ice cream

Method: blend the ingredients together until smooth.

 Chocolate

Glass: large highball
Garnish: none

1.5 fl oz chocolate syrup

1.5 fl oz milk

3 scoops of vanilla ice cream

Method: blend the ingredients together until the drink is smooth.

Chocolate chip

Glass large highball
Garnish: chocolate chips

2 tablespoons chocolate buttons/drops/chips

2 fl oz milk

3 scoops of vanilla ice cream

Method: blend the ingredients together until smooth.

■ Strawberry

Glass: large highball
Garnish: strawberry slice

4 fresh strawberries

2 fl oz milk

3 scoops of vanilla ice cream

Method: blend the ingredients together until smooth.

■ Vanilla

Glass: large highball
Garnish: none

0.25 fl oz vanilla extract

2.75 fl oz milk

3 scoops of vanilla ice cream

Method: blend the ingredients together until the drink is smooth.

◼ St Clements

Glass: large highball with ice
Garnish: none

2.5 fl oz bitter lemon

2.5 fl oz orange juice

Method: build the ingredients up straight into the glass.

◼ Tutti-frutti

Glass: large highball with ice
Garnish: none

1.5 fl oz orange juice

1.5 fl oz strawberry syrup

1 fl oz lemon juice

1 fl oz lime juice

Method: build the ingredients up straight into the glass, pouring the strawberry syrup in last. Then stir.

■ Shirley Temple

Glass: large highball with ice
Garnish: none

1 fl oz grenadine (non-alcoholic)

Top with lemonade

Method: pour the ingredients into the glass in the order listed and stir.

■ Virgin Mary

Glass: large highball with ice
Garnish: a lime squeeze/celery stick

5 fl oz Bloody Mary mix (see below)

Method: pour the ingredients into the glass over ice, stir.

Basic Bloody Mary mix
3.5 fl oz tomato juice
0.25 fl oz lemon juice
2 dashes Worcestershire sauce
2 drops Tabasco
Salt and pepper to taste

Variations: combine any or all of the following:
a) substitute celery salt for ordinary salt
b) substitute V8 juice for tomato juice
c) add a splash of beef bouillon.

Virgin colada

Glass: large highball with ice
Garnish: a pineapple slice/cherry

5 fl oz Pina-colada mix (see below)

Method: mix or blend the ingredients together and pour into the glass

Basic Pina-colada mix
3 fl oz pineapple juice

1 fl oz coconut cream

Variations: add any or all of the following and blend together to make a smooth mix for parties.
a) pineapple rings
b) orange juice or half and half
c) papaya cubes.